ADVENTURES IN THE GREAT OUTDOORS

CAMPING

ROBYN HARDYMAN

WINDMILL BOOKS
New York

Published in 2014 by Windmill Books, An Imprint of Rosen Publishing
29 East 21st Street, New York, NY 10010

Produced for Windmill by Calcium Creative Ltd
Editor for Calcium Creative Ltd: Sarah Eason
US Editor: Sara Howell
Designer: Emma DeBanks

Photo credits: Cover: Shutterstock: Kokhanchikov. Inside: Dreamstime: Alyssand 29,
Baldas1950 27, Crazygood40 9t, 9m, Fireflyphoto 24, Hallgerd 13, Jeffbanke 17,
Katseyephoto 20, Mathayward 14, Mikdam 26, Monkeybusinessimages 18, Paulmaguire
16t, Photosky 8, Russelllinton 19, Stargatechris 9b, Sutsaiy 22, Tbroucek 15, Zestmarina
21; Shutterstock: Lisa A 11, Claude Beaubien 7, Brocreative 6b, Cheryl Casey 10, Elena
Elisseeva 6t, gorillaimages 28t, 28b, Morgan Lane Photography 1, 5, 16b, 23, 25, Varina
and Jay Patel 12, Pavzyuk Svitlana 4.

Library of Congress Cataloging-in-Publication Data

Hardyman, Robyn.
Camping / by Robyn Hardyman.
pages cm. — (Adventures in the great outdoors)
Includes index.
ISBN 978-1-61533-747-7 (library binding) — ISBN 978-1-61533-811-5 (pbk.) —
ISBN 978-1-61533-812-2
1. Camping—Juvenile literature. I. Title.
GV191.7.H369 2014
796.54—dc23
2012049835

Manufactured in the United States of America

CPSIA Compliance Information: Batch #BS13WM: For Further Information contact Windmill Books, New York, New York at 1-866-478-0556

Contents

Go Wild!

It's time to get outside for a real adventure! When you leave the world of home, TV, computers, and school behind, you enter the amazing new world of nature. You're free to explore, to play, and to go wild!

Going on a camping trip is the perfect way to get in touch with the natural world and discover its wonders up close. You'll be sleeping under the stars, surrounded by the woods, or out on the beach with the sounds of the sea in your ears. Maybe you'll be in the mountains, with a huge **landscape** of nature laid out before you. How awesome is that?

You'll have an amazing ocean view if you camp on the beach.

A camping trip is a great way to make friends.

Camping gives you the chance to spend some time with your friends and family. You can play together, explore together, and cook and talk together. You'll learn new skills, too, such as **pitching** a **tent**, making a fire, or finding your way on a **hike**. Maybe you'll learn something about yourself, too. You might even find out that you're braver than you thought!

For a successful camping trip, you need to plan ahead, and think about where you want to go and what you will need. You also need to have a healthy attitude while you're in the wild. Let your imagination run wild, but always show respect for your **environment** and remember that it can be dangerous, too. That way, you'll be sure to have a wonderful adventure!

5

Plan Your Trip

You'll enjoy your camping trip far more if you have planned it well before you go. There is a lot to think about. What kind of **location** are you looking for? How long do you want to be away? What will the weather be like? Take time to answer these questions so you can find the perfect place to camp and plan what you need to take there.

The world is a big place! Are you headed for the beach, the woods, or the mountains? Will you be traveling far and staying long? More likely you'll be camping for just a few days in a location close to home. Do some research at home to find the perfect places for your trip. With an adult, look in books and on the Internet for great locations near you.

Researching locations together helps to get everyone in the mood for camping!

Hillside locations are quiet and peaceful places for camping.

Camping on large campsites with many other people can be noisy, but fun, too!

STAY SAFE!

Make sure the location you choose is free from **hazards** such as flooding or dangerous animals.

You can also choose between a campsite and the open countryside. If you choose to go to a campsite, find out which sites are best and if you need to make a reservation. Some campsites will not allow you to make a fire, so if you're dreaming of marshmallows and songs around a campfire at night, choose carefully! If you're going for a wild location, be sure to find out if camping is permitted.

Get the Gear

Having the right gear can make all the difference to the success of a camping trip. When it comes to camping equipment and **gadgets**, there is so much to choose! It's a good idea to get expert advice in a camping store. The most important items to choose are the right tent and a good **sleeping bag.**

Choose your tent carefully. Tents range from **lightweight**, single-person models, to large tents in which a whole family can sleep. Some tents can cope with extreme weather, while others are designed for more gentle use. Sleeping bags are rated by their warmth. If you're headed for the mountains, pick a warm one! To sleep comfortably, you'll need a **sleeping mat**, too.

A dome tent (pictured) is a good choice for two or three people, while a cabin-style tent gives you room to stand up.

STAY SAFE!

Don't forget to pack a first aid kit for emergencies and a flashlight for seeing in the dark.

Choose comfortable footwear to keep your feet dry and warm. Hiking boots are perfect if you're heading off on a hike.

Clothes are all about comfort and warmth when you're camping. Having several thin layers is best, so you can add more or take some off to suit the **temperature**. Keep your legs covered to protect yourself from scrapes and bugs, and wear comfortable shoes so you can easily get around. If you're going to be hiking, consider taking hiking shoes or boots, and a waterproof jacket.

If you're not making a real fire you'll need a stove for cooking, such as a portable gas stove. Take basic pans, plates, and utensils, and something to wash dishes in. A large container is useful for carrying water. Don't forget to plan what you're going to eat, and pack all the ingredients. Don't forget matches!

A sleeping mat makes sleeping on the ground much more comfortable.

We've Arrived!

You've found the perfect location. It may be on a fabulous beach, beside a lake, or deep in the woods. Wherever you are, be sure to choose a really great place to set up camp.

There are a few things to remember when picking your camping spot, whatever the type of landscape you're in. First, choose level ground. It's far more comfortable than a slope!

Next, you'll need a source of clean, flowing water nearby for drinking and washing. This is easy to find on a campsite. It can be more difficult in open countryside because you'll need to find a river or stream. Don't camp too close to water, though, or you might be at risk of flooding. Finally, you need a cooking area for your camp. This should be near the tents, but not too close, for fire safety.

STAY SAFE!

On the beach, make sure you set up camp away from the incoming tide.

Tents can be put up quite quickly, but be sure to practice before you camp.

Collecting Rainwater

You can drink pure rainwater while camping. Here's how!

You will need:
- large, clean container
- water purification tablets
- clean flask
- camp table

1 Position your table in an open area, away from any overhanging bushes or trees.

2 Place the container on the table.

3 After rainfall, collect the container and empty any rainwater into a clean flask.

4 Always boil your rainwater or add a water purification tablet to it before drinking it.

5 Enjoy your fresh, clean rainwater!

Pure rainwater tastes great if treated properly.

Keep Clean

Half the fun of living outdoors and having an adventure in the wild is getting dirty. It's all part of camping! However, it's still important to be able to get yourself and your gear clean at the end of the day.

At a campsite, water for washing and cooking is provided from a faucet. You'll need strong containers for carrying drinking water from the water source to your tent. In open country, you will have pitched camp close to a flowing water source such as a stream or river. **Stagnant** water, such as that in a pond, isn't safe to drink or to wash with. If you drink stagnant water, or swallow it while washing, it can make you very sick. Always head down to a stream to wash the dishes or collect water for cooking and drinking.

In the great outdoors it's okay to get a little dirty!

It's especially important to wash yourself, too, after a busy day exploring. It's easy to pick up **germs** when you're getting close to nature. Watch out, though, because the river water may be a little cold! Always wash your hands before you handle food or eat. If you are camping for more than a few days, you may need to wash some of your clothes, too. Hang them up to dry in the Sun and wind.

You don't want to **pollute** a natural water source with chemicals, so try to use as little soap as possible. Be sure to wash yourself and brush your teeth downstream from where you collect drinking water. That way you won't be drinking soapy water.

A morning wash in a cold stream will wake you up and get you ready for the day!

STAY SAFE! Streams and rivers can flow fast. Never get into the water to wash.

Ready for Fun

The camp's all set, and it's time for some fun! There are many great ways to have a good time outdoors, so get in touch with your wild side.

The shore, fields, and woods are full of great places to hang out. With sticks, mud, sand, stones, or leaves, you can make any number of tools and games. If you've prepared really well for your trip, you might even find you have a few extra items from home that can help to make great tools. Try making a **slingshot** from a Y-shaped stick and some thick elastic. Tie the elastic tightly around each arm of the fork. Or make a **blowpipe** by hollowing out the soft stem from a tree. Sharpen the end of a harder stick and use it to get the soft insides out of the soft stem.

STAY SAFE! Ask an adult to help you sharpen any sticks.

Explore your environment and discover an amazing natural playground.

Being able to read a map is a great skill to have for any outdoor trip.

Big groups can play some great games. Try "Capture the Flag." This is a game in which two teams each have a **territory**. You can mark the territory with some stones or branches, and you can use colored chalk to put the color of each team on the markers used. Each team must battle to take a "flag" from their **opponents**' territory, while still trying to **defend** their own territory!

You could even try setting up a treasure hunt, with lots of clues around camp. Try hiding items such as stones or sticks that you've marked with messages or clues about where the next find might be. Then ask your campmates to find the treasure!

Nature Watch

Camping is one of the best ways to get close to nature, and the great outdoors is packed with cool places to explore and awesome animals to see.

If you're camping in the woods, look up in the trees to see all the birds and animals living around you. On the ground, piles of leaves and rotting logs make great homes for bugs. Use a magnifying glass to see really up-close. If you're near a river or lake, lie flat on the ground near the water. See what's swimming in the depths, or skimming the surface.

You can see different things at different times of day. Many creatures prefer to come out in the early morning or evening. Look for different animal tracks and different kinds of animal waste, too.

Deer can be found by looking for the tracks they leave.

A walk in the woods is a great way to hunt for bugs.

Tracking Animals

Animals are all around you outdoors. You can find them by following the track marks they leave behind.

1 Look all around you for any signs of track marks in the mud or leaves, or broken twigs on the bushes and trees.

2 If you see a track mark, try to identify it using your guidebook.

3 Follow where the track mark leads, then use your binoculars to see if you can spot the animal.

Explore This!

You will need:
- animal track guidebook
- binoculars

Look for animal tracks in wet dirt or sand.

STAY SAFE! Always make sure you have an adult with you while tracking animals.

17

Hiking and Fishing

While you're out in the wild, why not explore even further by going for a hike? Hiking is a great way to see the wilderness up close, and it's great exercise, too. If you prefer, you could go fishing and catch your own dinner! There is always a lot of wildlife around wild, watery places, so while you are fishing, look out for animals and plants around you.

To make the most of your hike, put on your hiking boots, pack some water and a map in a small backpack, and head off into the wild! You can see so much more when you're on the move. Listen for the birds, and look carefully all around you to see nature in action. Don't forget to take an animal identification guidebook and camera with you. That way you'll be able to figure out which animals you've seen and take photos of them, too.

STAY SAFE! Always go hiking with an adult and stay on marked paths.

See nature up close on a hike.

Fish near your camp to learn a new skill, watch the wildlife, and bring back dinner!

If you're camping near water, take time out for some fishing. You'll need some basic gear, such as a **fishing rod** and line, some **bait**, a hook and a bobber, and a net. With an adult, first check that fishing's permitted, then find a good place to fish. This may be shady water under trees or a still pool. Cast your line into the water and wait. You'll be amazed at all the wildlife you see as you sit still. Release your catch back into the water, or cook it for dinner!

19

The Campfire

A great campfire is the heart of camp. Everyone loves the scent of wood smoke, the crackle of logs, and the flickering flames. You can gather around your campfire to eat, sing, or tell stories.

To make your campfire, start by clearing an area of all **debris**. Make a ring of rocks to surround your fire. You need three kinds of material to burn. First, find tiny twigs, dry grass, bark, or wood shavings, to light the fire. Second, you need small, dry sticks, called **kindling**. These will burn easily. Finally, collect larger sticks and logs to burn for a longer time. Collect all three kinds, and stack them in piles away from the fire site.

This kind of fire pit takes longer to make, but it will burn for a long time. You can also use it more than once.

Make a loose pile of the dry twigs and grass in the middle of the ring. With your back to the wind, strike a match and light the pile. Put the match in the pile, too. You may need to blow on it gently to get it going. Once it's burning, add small pieces of kindling. The wood can be either stacked up in a tepee shape, or crisscrossed in a pile. Either way, be sure that air can always get into the base. When the fire is really going well, add the larger logs, one at a time. Place more large logs around the fire for everyone to sit on.

Let the fire burn down to ash, and then put it out completely. Scatter the ashes and sprinkle with water. Drench any charred logs.

A carefully-made fire can burn for several hours.

STAY SAFE!

Never make a fire under trees or in windy conditions. It could easily spread out of control.

Make a Feast

It's evening time and everyone is hungry. It's time for food! Campsite food is best kept simple so it's easy to make on camping cooking equipment.

You will have decided at home on your method for cooking. It may be a grill over an open fire, a pan over a portable gas stove, or simply some wooden skewers to hold over the campfire flames. You can cook most fish, meat, and vegetables with this simple equipment. Be sure that your food and equipment have been thoroughly washed before you start to cook.

STAY SAFE!

Always ask an adult to handle the hot food and pans.

Foods taste especially good when they're cooked and eaten outdoors.

Campfire Cook

Explore This!

Marshmallows toasted on an open fire make the best camping snack ever.

1 Once your campfire is lit, carefully press a marshmallow onto the end of a long stick.

2 Hold the marshmallow toward the fire or just above the flames.

3 Toast the marshmallow for a few seconds until it is warm, gooey, and ready to eat!

You will need:
- campfire
- marshmallows
- long sticks for toasting

Toast gooey marshmallows as evening falls.

23

Fun After Dark

As evening comes, and you're feeling a little sleepy, hang out around the campfire. Make the most of having no TV and no computers. Telling stories around the campfire and singing songs are great ways to have fun instead.

The wilderness gets really wild at night, too, when different animals come out. You may not be able to see them, but there are other ways of telling they are there. Listen for the call of owls in the darkness or the rustle of rabbits, deer, and mice in the bushes.

Lots of insects come out at night, too. In the evening, you'll find that some amazing bugs are attracted by your camp lights. You might see fireflies, too. These awesome creatures are actually beetles with wings, and they produce flashes of light at night that light up the darkness around you.

Fireflies give off an awesome light at night.

Try making scary shadows against your tent walls to really scare each other!

As the last light fades, you can try making up spooky stories to thrill and chill you in the dark! One person starts the story off with a scary sentence. The next person adds another sentence. Scared yet? Continue around the campfire two or three times to finish the story. Or how about a "truth or dare" session? Each person has to tell a secret about themselves or accept a dare.

If things get too spooky, change the mood with some campfire singing. Make your songs silly and fun until everyone's laughing. Songs like "Boom Chicka Boom" can go on for hours and hours!

Starry Night

Sleeping out under the stars is amazing. There is nothing above you but the enormous sky and the stars twinkling far away, deep in space.

It's totally dark, you're out in the wild, and you're **connected** with nature like never before. The sounds and smells of the outdoors are more intense than ever. Can you see the moon hanging in the sky, casting silvery moon shadows over everything around you?

While camping in the wild, there are no street lights or pollution fumes to fog up the night sky. This makes it a great time for stargazing.

Enjoy the peace of the night after all your adventures in the wild.

Stargazing

Gazing up at the stars is the perfect
way to end a day's camping.

You will need:
- huge, clear sky
  full of stars
- binoculars
- guidebook on the
  constellations

1 Gather together in sleeping bags, with heads
close together and bodies fanned out in
a circle, like the spokes of a bicycle wheel.

2 Turn off any lights you have shining in camp.
They make it harder to see the stars.

3 Once your eyes have gotten used to the dark,
try to find patterns in the stars.

4 Take turns to look through the binoculars.
You'll see thousands of stars!

5 One person can look up a few
constellations, or star groups,
in the guidebook, and point
them out to the others.

6 If you're really lucky, you
may see a shooting star.

*Look up into the night sky.
What can you see?*

Go Green

We all have a responsibility to keep our wild places safe and unspoiled for the future. That way, everyone can continue to enjoy them. Whatever your outdoor adventure, remember to respect the natural world and make as little impact on it as you can.

Leaving litter, camping equipment, or food behind can spoil a beautiful, natural space and harm the wildlife that live there. Remember, whatever you take with you on your camping trip needs to be taken back home again!

Having a great camping adventure is all about looking, discovering, and enjoying, but not disturbing your location. There are several things to think about when you try to leave no trace behind. While you're having fun in the woods, for example, don't carve on tree trunks. Never write graffiti anywhere, though writing your name in the sand on the beach, to be washed away by the sea, is just fine!

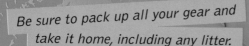

Be sure to pack up all your gear and take it home, including any litter.

Leave the landscape as beautiful as you found it so that others can come and enjoy it, too.

Leave behind the plants and flowers you discover so that others can enjoy them, too. And it's never wise to chase, feed, or try to pet any animals you come across, even if they are really tiny! Wild animals are meant to be wild, so never try to treat them like a pet.

When it's time to pack up, be sure to take your gear home with you, including any litter. The idea is to leave your location as clean as you found it. Or, if it wasn't very clean, clean it up for future adventurers. If you leave no trace behind you, no one else will ever know you were there!

Glossary

bait (BAYT) Food that is put on a hook to catch fish.

blowpipe (BLOH-pyp) A tube for shooting out pellets by blowing.

connected (kuh-NEKT-ed) Tied to or having to do with.

constellations (kon-stuh-LAY-shunz) Groups of stars.

debris (duh-BREE) Garbage.

defend (dih-FEND) To protect.

environment (en-VY-ern-ment) All the living things and conditions of a place.

fishing rod (FISH-ing RAWD) A long pole with a line attached for fishing.

gadgets (GA-jets) Mechanical equipment.

germs (JERMZ) Tiny organisms that can cause disease.

hazardz (HA-zerdz) Dangers or risks, such as flooding or wild animals.

hike (HYK) A long walk.

kindling (KIHND-ling) Small pieces of wood used to start a fire.

landscape (LAND-skayp) A large, wild area.

lightweight (LYT-wayt) Not heavy.

location (loh-KAY-shun) A place, such as a camping place.

opponents (uh-POH-nents) People who are against you.

pitching (PIH-ching) Putting up a tent.

pollute (puh-LOOT) To make dirty, or to harm by adding chemicals.

sleeping bag (SLEEP-ing BAG) A padded bag to sleep in while camping.

sleeping mat (SLEEP-ing MAT) A thin, soft mat to sleep on.

slingshot (SLING-shot) A device with elastic for shooting objects.

stagnant (STAG-nint) Water that does not flow, but is still.

temperature (TEM-pur-cher) How hot or cold something is.

tent (TENT) A shelter that can be put up and taken down easily.

territory (TER-uh-tor-ee) An area a person or animal considers to be their own or belonging to them.

Further Reading

Brunelle, Lynn. *Camp Out!: The Ultimate Kids' Guide*.
  New York: Workman Publishing Group, 2008.

Champion, Neil. *Camping and Hiking*. Get Outdoors.
  New York: PowerKids Press, 2011.

Howard, Melanie A. *Camping For Kids*. Into the Great
  Outdoors. Mankato, MN: Capstone Press, 2013.

Rey, H. A. *Find the Constellations*. New York:
  Houghton Mifflin Company, 2009.

Websites

For web resources related to the subject of this book, go to:
www.windmillbooks.com/weblinks and select this book's title.

Index